Enough is Enough

Creator and illustrator: Patrick Arguin

English translation: Bleu Dactylo

French version written by: Michèle Rappe
Support, coaching and collaboration: Hélène Beaudette

I want to offer my deepest gratitude to Hélène Beaudette.
Her unconditional support and presence allowed TOOLS OF THE HEART to grow and come into form.

After a long morning of pouring rain, the sun is finally back! Fluffy is happy to stretch his legs and climb up on Colin's head to greet the sun.

Colin is a little tired and would gladly
just bask in the sun quietly.

But Fluffy wants to play!
He climbs, leaps, and slides everywhere!

The squirrel is now swinging cheerfully.
Colin is happy to see that his friend is so joyful,
but he really would enjoy some time alone.

«Maybe Fluffy will soon get tired and stop,
and I will be able to rest,» thinks Colin.

However, Fluffy has discovered a new game; he bounces and jumps on Colin's branches as if it was a trampoline. Colin is starting to feel irritated and hopes that Fluffy's games will soon end.

«STOP!»
Colin suddenly shouts.
«You're not fun anymore!
You are jumping everywhere,
and I'm tired of it!»

Fluffy freezes.
«Why are you shouting like this?» he says.
«You are not fun either!» And the squirrel
retreats inside Colin's trunk.

Colin is mad. «Fluffy does not listen to me,» he thinks.
«I just wanted some peace and quiet!»

Longing to feel calm again, Colin takes deep long
breaths and goes into his heart to find his rainbow
of wisdom. He feels a bright light growing, and a
familiar silhouette appears before him.

«Dear Colin,» says Purple, «do you think Fluffy knew that you needed rest?» «I told him to stop because he was annoying me!» says Colin.

Purple invites the oak to recall the details of the situation. Colin remembers. «No,» he says. «Before I yelled, Fluffy did not know I wanted calm.»

«Sometimes,» says Purple, «it's difficult to say what we really want, and we hope that the other person will guess it.»

Colin admits that instead of talking to his friend, he waited for him to guess his needs. «I was afraid to talk because I did not want to make him sad.»

«You see Colin, it might seem difficult to speak up, even to a friend, but to stay silent is not the answer.»

«Keeping quiet and not expressing your needs can create many uncomfortable emotions and misunderstandings.»

«That's true,» Colin thinks, «I said nothing and kept getting more and more furious.»

«What is important,» says the elf, «is to express yourself with respect. When you see your friend, talk to him about what happened.»

Colin feels a soft purple light in him. He feels peaceful again and opens his eyes.

«Purple is right! Fluffy is a true friend, and if I tell him I need to be alone sometimes, he will understand. I will talk to him!» decides Colin.

«Fluffy, Fluffy... can you hear me?»
The squirrel sticks his head out carefully.

«I would like to talk to you,» says Colin.
Fluffy climbs onto a branch.

«I'm sorry I yelled at you like that, I got
carried away. Are you mad at me?»

Fluffy thinks for a moment: «No,» he says,
«I am not mad, but I don't like it when you
shout at me like that.»

«I appreciate you a lot Colin, but it really
bothers me when you react this way.
I did not understand what was
happening to you.»

«I'm truly sorry Fluffy. It won't happen again!
I know now that it is better to say how I feel and
what I want, rather than let others guess it!»

Fluffy chuckles and hugs his dear friend!

When Father Sun sets on the horizon, Fluffy and Colin gaze upon the many colors of the garden, with the sky displaying its beautiful shades of orange, red and purple.

Remember...

What can I do when I feel misunderstood?
The people around you cannot guess what you are feeling or what you need. It is important that you openly express yourself clearly to make sure they understand you.

How can I openly express my feelings?
When something displeases you, talk about how you feel, what you want and what you are going through during that situation. When something pleases you, express it as well!

Why is it important to explain how I feel?
When you say how you feel, you help your friends understand you better. Let's say you need some time alone when your friends want to play; it's better to tell them how you feel, rather than getting mad at them or doing something you don't feel like doing. That way, you are taking care of yourself.

The Book Collection

Tools of the Heart
Fostering Confidence and Self-esteem

1 Father Sun and Mother Earth Create Life
Breathing/Finding your rhythm

Breathing is essential to life; conscious breathing is a simple, yet effective way to regain your calm and well-being by finding your body's rhythm.

2 Fluffy and the Rainbow in his Heart
Meditation/Finding your inner calm

Each one of us has a peaceful place inside their heart. Meditation is a tool that allows you to find your personal space or to go back to it.

3 Colin Discovers Confidence
Grounding/Strengthening your self-confidence

Growing up often comes with its share of fears and hesitations. Growing solid roots helps to build and nurture a positive self-confidence.

4 Colin and Fluffy Become Friends
Knowing yourself/Loving and appreciating

Positive self-confidence and self-esteem are the building blocks of healthy relationships; therefore, learning to appreciate who we are is a treasure for life.

5 The Choice
Insight/Listening to your intuition

Learning to listen to your inner voice and how to trust it, is learning to stay true to yourself in all situations.

6 Colin's Courage
Expressing/Confidence in yourself

Standing up for yourself is not wrong. It is about relying on your self-worth with confidence, to respectfully say what you need to say.

7 Enough is Enough
Self-respect/Daring to be yourself

Developing good communication skills also implies expressing your feelings and needs in a respectful manner, which can sometimes be a challenge!

8 Fluffy Finds his Well-being
Self-awareness/Taking responsibility

Growing up is also about becoming more aware of your emotions and learning to manage them responsibly.

The Meditation Collection

Tools of the Heart
Fostering Confidence and Self-esteem

Specially designed for young children, the guided meditations explore and develop the same themes, as seen in the **Tools of the Heart** book collection. These intend to reinforce the children's knowledge of themselves through their inner space of wisdom, where things can be seen, heard, and felt.

Meditation is also a wonderful tool that children can easily learn to help them self-regulate physically, mentally, and emotionally.

To learn more, go to our website:

www.toolsoftheheart.com

www.ingramcontent.com/pod-product-compliance
Lightning Source LLC
Chambersburg PA
CBHW041158120626
46547CB00020B/3256